Today is the best day of my life thus far.

I am closer to living my dreams than I have ever been.

J. H. Wright

Rethinking Failure

J. H. Wright

Copyright © 2018 J. H. Wright

Published and distributed in the United States

All rights reserved. No parts of this book may be reproduced by any mechanical, photographic, or electronic process, or in the form of a photographic recording; nor may it be stored in a retrieval system, transmitted or otherwise be copied for public or private use. The exception would be in the case of brief quotations, embodied in the critical articles or reviews or pages where permission is specifically granted by the publisher or author.

Unauthorized reproduction of any part of this work is illegal and is punishable by law.

Ordering Information

This book may be purchased for business, or sales promotional use. For information, please e-mail creditdefendersm@yahoo.com or write to CREDITDEFENDER^{SM}, P. O. Box 2405, Cedar hill, TX 75106

FIRST EDITION

Library of Congress Control Number:

ISBN-13: 978-1-949820-00-3

All passages are the sole thoughts and viewpoints of the author based on his ideals and individual expertise and experience. Any principals and philosophical information should not be considered medical, legal, mental health or otherwise.

This book is dedicated to every person that dares to become independent, happy, and free from the past.

To those not intimidated by stepping into destiny and truth.

To all those who have inspired me whether intentionally, or not with the determination to press forward.

And most importantly to my daughter, who has always been the purpose I have needed to be a better person.

To others who still feel lost, know that you are not forgotten. It is my pleasure to share with you three very basic principals that will change your life. I present to you this book as a first step in helping you find your personal road to happiness and success.

ACKNOWLEDGMENTS

Not withstanding the efforts of myself, the success of writing this book has largely depended on the encouragement and leadership of others who had faith in me. I take this opportunity to express my gratitude to those who have been instrumental in the implementation, and completion of this project.

I thank Craig Wilson who in hope that I might discover the delights that can arise from the pitfalls of life, encouraged me to read my very first motivational book.

Cherise, because you believed I had something to say, your unwaiving support inspired me to share my personal experiences.

I must also recognize Mrs. Whitaker, Miss Bethune, and Mrs. Warren, educators who expected more from me, and taught me to play by different rules.

I would like to show my greatest appreciation to Dr. Henry Clifford Kinley, for his words of wisdom. Without his guidance I would not have been able to accomplish this task. He motivates and encourages me in everything that I do.

The support I have received from others who contributed and who are contributing to this project, has also been vital for creation of this book. It has been a long journey, and you have given me strength when times were most difficult. I am grateful for your constant friendship, and trust that I will make you proud.

CONTENTS

Chapters:	Page
1) What Is Failure	1
2) Closed Doors vs. Open Minds	3
3) Discovering Your Norm	7
4) Promoting Yourself	13
5) Rise, Fall, and Rise Again	16
6) Unexpected Rewards	22
7) Process of Elimination	27
8) Strategic Planning	29
9) Making The Grade	33
10) Curing Mental Roadblocks	36
11) Art Of The Self Sell	40
12) Trash Can Become Your Treasure	46
13) The Experiment	63
14) The Enemy Within	68
15) Writing Your Own Script	73
16) Upping The Ante	79
17) Perfecting Your Balance	87
18) Enjoying The Victory	92
19) Epilogue	94
About The Author	

CHAPTER 1
WHAT IS FAILURE

ASK ANYONE THIS QUESTION, and you're bound to get answers that sound pretty much alike. Throughout mankind, this has been one of the dirtiest, if not the dirtiest word in any person's language or vocabulary. We generally think of failure has something to avoid at all cost. When was the last time you heard someone proudly proclaim that they had failed at anything? After all, why would anyone want to fail?

According to Merriam-Webster's dictionary, some definitions of failure include: a state of inability to perform a nomal function, lack of success, falling short of.

It also list synonyms such as: default, delinquency, poverty, dereliction, neglect, negligence, and oversight, to name a few.

Any of these sound familiar, or as a desirable trait you would want to have?

Well, what if we looked at the definition from a different perspective? What if we use this dirty little word to our advantage. What if we could make it work for us rather than against us?

While this may sound quite unreasonable, maybe even mad, let's remember there was a time when for many hundreds of years people accepted the notion that the world was flat. They thought the sun revolved around the earth, and if you ventured to far you'd fall over the edge or be consumed by monstrous creatures.

Well I'm here to declare to you that the word failure has in fact received a bad reputation. I am going to show just how important failure has not only been to mankind, but more importantly how valuable it can be to you.

I will show why you should not only rethink your failures, but why you should expect and explore them. Then as we progress forward, I will guide you through the process of making your failures work to your advantage. If you want a life that is barely recognizable from your current plight, then this book is for you. I will show you exactly how to use your failures as milestones to take you precisely, where you want to go. I will guide you as you begin living a life of abundance. Together we will open doors to new possibilities. Possibilities that you may have thought were out of reach will not only become attainable, but will become your reality.

CHAPTER 2
CLOSED DOORS VS. OPEN MINDS

First, let me say, you will recognize yourself as you continue reading or listening to audio of this book. There is no one ever born, where these laws, these principals, these rules do not apply. Therefore seeing that failures are an inescapable part of life, let us learn new ways of viewing them.

I personally came to realize what value can come from failure whether early in life. However, only recently did I ever associate just how important it is to my success. I did know that through failure, I had learned a few things, but I didn't fully realize that for every success, there usually were a number of proceeding failures. These series of failures, whatever they have been, always managed to spring me forward. As I look back, I find that my outcome or success was always far bigger and better than it was before the challenges or so called "failures."

In other words, Newton's Third Law of Motion, "For every action, there is an equal and opposite reaction." So, if that is law and if that is true, it stands to reason that the greater the setback, the challenge, the "failure," the greater the returning status quo, the endurance, the success.

Now don't get me wrong, it's not that I enjoy my failures. Nor do I welcome them with open invitations. However, when they do happen, as they will, I now have the tools to move through the valley of despair without pitching a tent and staying there.

I've developed the tools to envision what's over the mountain, and the confidence to make the climb.

When we look at our heroes, our sheroes, our athletes, entertainers, entrepreneurs, and other successful people, what we usually tend to focus on are their victories, their successes, their accomplishments. Seldom do we really delve into their journey to see how they got to these prestigious positions. In our minds we see them just as people who have more likely than not experienced a few tough times in life, but fate has been kind, smiled down on them and their circumstances were somehow better than our own.

However, if we take a closer look, we will find that more times then not they have suffered great challenges in areas of life that we all have in common.

Take for example did you know that Harland David Sanders was fired from various jobs before founding what is now known as the "KFC" empire. The great Oprah Winfrey was publicly fired from her first television job, as an anchor in Baltimore.

Steven Spielberg was rejected by the University of Southern California School of Cinematic Arts, more than once. Walt Disney was fired as a cartoonist, because it was said he "lacked imagination and had no good ideas."

Image that, some of the most creative minds either being rejected or told they had no good ideas. The list goes on and on.

Has it ever happened to you or someone that you know? How was the failure and the humiliation handled? Did the rebound take you to a better place? Or did you regress into a dark space where you have yet to escape? Or have you escaped only to settle for just getting back on your feet again, meaning in essence you haven't escaped at all. You're just caught in the trap and have conveniently accepted this has your plight.

Now before you start thinking, well these people were extremely gifted or talented, while that is undoubtedly true, we cannot let ourselves off so easily. The truth is we all to various degrees, have some talent, and when we look at our personal lives, are we really living up to our potential? If not, why not?

CHAPTER 3
DISCOVERING YOUR NORM

WILLIAM JAMES SAID, "Compared to what we ought to be, we are only half awake. We are making use of only a small part of our physical and mental resources. Stating the thing broadly, the human individual thus lives far within his limits. He possesses power of various sorts which he habitually fails to use."

In essence, we only utilize a portion of our talents. When we deny development of these talents, we not only cheat ourselves, but we also cheat the world.

Is it because we are afraid of failure and without realizing it we are living failure every day simply because we avoid stepping away from our comfort zone? Do we look at our personal lives with the same scrutiny that we look at our neighbors, our friends, our family?

Are we more critical of ourselves and less forgiving for our own mistakes than we are for others?

RETHINKING FAILURE

We tell a friend, don't give up on relationships just because you've been hurt. But we then do just the opposite by sabotaging our relationships based on some hurtful experience we've had in the past.

When our neighbor loses his or her job, we tell them to keep the faith, the market is tough, but I'm sure you'll find something soon. But when it happens to us, we take it out on our mates, our children, kick the dog, and say my life is in the toilet.

Does any of this sound familiar? Well strap in and hold on tight because I have just begin the process of getting us to rethink failure.

You see, you must rethink failure and your relationship with it, because the universe has it's own way of making us repeat a thing until we learn the lesson. Think of the universe as a gigantic classroom, you are it's student, if you cannot do the homework and pass the exam, there is no choice but to repeat the course.

Have you ever noticed that whatever your pain is, it's probably shown up before in some other scenario, perhaps under some other guise?

Take for example the person that relocates from place to place because according to their way of thinking, there are no good people in their locale which they can establish a meaningful and a committed relationship. They go from one failed relationship to another. They are angry, they are tired, they are sad. However, if they'd look behind the scene, they may just discover that the problem has not been the relationships. In all likelihood, there is an underling characteristic that they are carrying from relationship to relationship that will only be resolved by rethinking these failures and the part they themselves have played.

Or maybe you find yourself living a life that is far different than the one you'd perceived when you were in your youth. You started out strong, but somewhere along the way you settled in to the norm. Now let's be clear here, I'm not talking about your "norm," but the "norm" that society, your neighbors, your friends, your family, convinced you to live within. Remember, your "norm," was the life you'd perceived. What is the norm for you, is not the norm for anyone else simply because you are unique.

Yes, there are certain rules, laws, guidelines, whatever we choose to call them, that must exist in order for society to function. But to often we use them to justify staying within our comfort zones.

I'm not suggesting that our failures should be pleasant, nor am I suggesting we should always throw caution to the wind. I'm only saying that life is never going to be easy, so if we are to enjoy the time we have on this planet, we must learn the art of recovering from situations so that they lead us where we desire to go, and not where the circumstance itself suggests we should be. It is a law of nature that only the strong survive. That law in itself suggests that we are all going to face challenges.

One definition of the word challenge is, "a call out to duel or combat," but whatever definition you choose to use, it infers something most likely that requires being a bit uncomfortable. Whether you apply the word to work, sports, relationships, education, or any life experience, that's just the way it is.

Did you know that your brain is like a muscle? The more you use it, the more you exercise it, the more you expect from it, the more efficient it becomes. You are a marvelous work of mastery. Anything you can envision and hold to with real conviction is able to become your reality.

Let's back up a bit. Let's go back to a failure we all can relate to and see how our mind processed it. As an infant, there came a point in time when you were presented with one of the most basic challenges, the challenge to stop crawling on the floor, and to walk on two legs.

Now while this may seem completely natural, let's exam the actual thought process. You looked around and at some point realized, "hey other folks are not sliding across the floor, they are moving in a way that seems more comfortable, more appealing." You then concluded in your mind even before you attempted to walk, that you would walk. You didn't question what other's thought, nor did you know exactly how you would achieve the goal.

You only knew at this point, that it looked more pleasant, and that you were going to accomplish the feat. You actually believed, and envisioned that you would walk before you took the first steps. At some point, and with courage, you decided to pull up by a table, a chair, or some other object, and to move your legs forward.

Undoubtedly, you fell down several times, but did it register in your mind as a "failure?" I seriously doubt it, although by definition of the way we use the word, this was one of, if not your first failure in life. And even though you failed, you got praises, claps, and hugs, from your parents for making this effort. You did not feel ashamed, nor did anyone scold you. Why, because this is what society expected. Therefore what is actually one of our earliest failures in life was processed in our brains in such a way that it became an asset instead of a liability.

You envisioned yourself walking upright, and society expected and said it was okay for you to walk. So you stepped away from your comfort zone of crawling on the floor, and your brain automatically programmed the information needed in order for you to get your balance and bring what was a goal into realty.

Had society done the opposite and

continually made you feel embarrassed or less than, and you'd accepted that "truth," in all likelihood you would have never accomplished this simple feat.

We will look deeper into other scenarios as we move forward, but as you can plainly see here, it was because of the way you viewed the failure as well as the way society perceived the failure that determined how you were affected.

CHAPTER 4
PROMOTING YOURSELF

THERE ARE NUMEROUS OBSTACLES that we as humans have learned to overcome and use to not only survive, but to form viable and magnificent societies. However, as we tend to develop beyond those youthful years of innocence, society also has it's way of placing limits on the individual that may be in conflict with our dreams, our talents, the expectations that we want from life.

We look at our present circumstances and often consider them to be acceptable only because others have conditioned our minds into thinking that we are not talented enough, smart enough, strong enough, maybe even good enough to push beyond any limits they themselves have in their minds. We become so influenced by family, friends, and co-workers that we don't want to appear weak. So we therefore settle into mediocrity without ever realizing that we are settling into failure.

My position is, if we must experience failure anyway, instead of settling into it, why not use it to build a foundation upon which we can analyze these failures, then set larger goals, and use the failures as milestones to move us closer toward some greater good.

The most successful salesperson is the one who predetermines through visualization, that he or she has the best product or service. They have something people want, and they know how to deliver it. Therefore, with confidence they will promote the product or service, and is rewarded by means of money, promotions, awards, vacations, and many such other desirable treasures. Obviously knowing that not everyone will buy, the super salesperson does realize that each no will get them closer to the desired yes. They refuse to allow the denials to be viewed as failure, but instead as milestones toward an ultimate goal or achievement.

You must see yourself as a salesperson, and what you are selling is yourself. Your abilities, your talents, your beliefs, your dreams. You must therefore, like the salesperson who is selling a product or service, visualize the life you desire and constantly hold that vision in your mind until it is so detailed and clear that it actually begins to take on shape and form.

You will often hear successful people say that their vision of success was so strong they could actually feel and live it in their mind, even before it materialized. Such commitment is a vital part of giving you the drive you will need in order to stay the coarse. You must also accept the reality that the larger or more challenging your dream, the greater the obstacles you're likely to encounter along the way.

But if you see yourself as "selling" yourself, and not just buying what other's are selling you, like the super salesperson, you will move with confidence, assured that you have something of value. And when obstacles arise, that assurance will give you the courage needed to press forward against the tide.

CHAPTER 5
RISE, FALL, AND RISE AGAIN

YEARS AGO WHEN I was just coming into adulthood, I like so many others wanted to embrace all that life had to offer. I'd been fortunate enough to find what was considered a good job at a major international company. I had a family and was on my way to living what I thought was the American dream. We had a comfortable home in a middle class neighborhood, three vehicles in the driveway, and all the trappings that many people considered as quite remarkable for someone who was not yet twenty years of age. Yes, in a very short time, I'd pulled myself up from an impoverished childhood, to responsible adulthood.

I was breaking all the rules. Most considered it would lead to my destruction. My friends went off to college, I chose to get a job, start a family, and go to community college at night. I had a clear picture of what I wanted my life to be like, and was formulating a plan to get me there.

I was moving at rapid speed, but just as great as my rise would be my fall. It was less than five years into the marriage when everything completely caved in on me. Like a domino effect, the marriage failed, I became unemployed, which than led to foreclosure on my home, and having the vehicles repossessed.

Things were absolutely awful. I was over my head in debt, unemployed, and completely on my own. Before the age of twenty five, I had risen and fallen. I was confused, and naturally unhappy.

The only thing that seemed to matter was that I now had a child, and that was my inspiration to figure a way out. I had to make my life work, and work successfully so that I could be an example.

This was important to me, because I had been brought up on welfare by a single mother. I had always felt ashamed, and less than. That feeling was reinforced by constantly being reminded that there were just certain things poor people shouldn't expect, and to add insult to injury the fact that I was black was not going to be of help.

I did not want my child to ever feel there were any limits that could not be reached. I refused to allow that same pattern of poverty, and negative thinking to continue because of my actions. I knew there had to be an answer, and that answer was not going to come from what others might consider to be logical. I would not file bankruptcy, nor would I become dependent on social services, move back home, or any of the options that were conveniently offered at the time.

I attempted several multi-level marketing ventures, none of which worked for me. However, I did learn two critical steps towards anyone's success. I learned that first you must have a clear vision of what you want to accomplish, and secondly, you must be resilient. In other words, you must expect and be able to rebound from disappointment and/or failure.

I decided I would take what I had learned from those multi-level ventures, and not only apply that knowledge to my business life, but also to my personal life. I committed not only to redesign my thought process, but also to redesign my life.

I made the gut wrenching decision to relocate halfway across the country, and to reinvent the person that I was. The greatest challenge I saw as an absent parent, focused on remaining active, constant and supportive in my child's life. To this end, I committed to a bond of mutual respect, trust, and love as a priority and felt anything else was completely achievable.

So selling whatever remaining possessions that I had, I bought a one way ticket and took off without really knowing exactly what I would be facing. I had no job offers, no place to live, and no idea how I would make things work.

But what I did have was a vision, and belief. I envisioned a different life, I believed I could succeed. And I laid out a plan to not only do it, but to do it on my own terms.

Grasping the significance of what being lay-off had done, how it had stripped my material possessions away from me, I was determined that I would not allow another company to have that much control over my life. Therefore, I set in motion a plan of action. That plan would allow me to temporarily get hired into another major company with the sole purpose of remaining there only long enough to get back on my feet again. Once that goal was met, I would leave the job and start my own business, which by the way, I had no idea what that business might be.

From the day I started that job, I had a date for several years later, marked on my calendar that I would quit. It was the risk I was willing to take in order to remove the dependency of someone else deciding just how far I could go in life.

Everything was going so well. The job was professional, offered great benefits, and the pay was comparable. I admit, I had no complaints whatsoever. But that did not stop me. I actually quit the job approximately two years prior to my targeted date.

I remember very clearly marching into my supervisor's office and announcing that I was giving notice. He naturally assumed I had gotten a better offer elsewhere. But when he asked about it, I replied, I had no idea what I would be doing, to which he was utterly shocked.

I however was very serious and being very honest. All that I knew for certain, was that I would never complete another job application or submit a resume to work for anyone else. My perspective was that whatever they paid me, was obviously less then I was worth, otherwise they could not profit from my service.

I thought, why should they make a profit off my work, and then give me just a cut of that profit, when I could keep it all if I was courageous enough to cut out the middleman?

As it had taken this plan several years to develop, I had once again purchased a new home, had a couple new vehicles, and was now living the very comfortable, and carefree life of being single. It would have been so easy for me remain at that job, but my vision just would not allow me to be satisfied.

I decided that before quitting I would pay off one of the vehicles, so that if things did not work out, I would live in the car, but I would not seek employment by any means. I was determined to make it on my own initiative. This would turn out to be one of my greatest challenges, but also one of my greatest rewards.

CHAPTER 6
UNEXPECTED REWARDS

EVERYONE WAS EAGER to express just how foolish my decision was. They didn't understand how or why I would risk so much when it seemed life had handed me such a gift. A gift that I was walking away from to pursue a dream, although I had no idea just how I was going to do it.

They felt life had given me a second chance, and here I was deliberately jumping out of an airplane with no parachute, so to speak of.

My reasoning however told me that if I had absolutely no income, it would not only force me to be disciplined enough to create a plan, work that plan, and manage my time constructively, but also force me into finding a business idea that would work for me.

After about a year of quitting the job, I once again found myself in the same situation as I had years earlier. I had virtually depleted all monies I'd reserved as a safety net until I could build a business. And once again, I had built up massive debt. The mortgage was delinquent, and I was robbing Peter to pay Paul.

Yes, before the age of thirty-five, I had now risen and fallen twice. As I was sitting one day, I saw someone walking around my property. When I inquired, they informed me that my home was to be auctioned off in less than a week. And although I was well aware I was behind in the mortgage, the mortgage company itself had failed to inform me that they would no longer work with me, nor had they told me of the auction.

Now by all accounts, you might say that I had failed rather early in life, and I admit, I thought I had. You see I still didn't grasp the notion that failure could actually be a positive experience if I viewed it from a different perspective. All I knew at the time was that once again, I had to somehow get back on my feet. I didn't really analyze my failures in a positive sense. I don't exactly know how I viewed them, but I do know I did not associate them in anyway to the success that would later follow.

What I did do was take time to reason out a plan. I decided to find a cheap apartment in a more centrally located part of town. And with only about three days before the auction, I packed, got moved, and continued trying to create a business that would work.

I attempted and put aside several business ideas before almost by accident discovering the one that would lead to my success.

You see having been through financial ruin twice, if nothing else I'd learned and figured out ways to get myself out of debt without filing bankruptcy or dealing with the issue of negative information staying on my credit reports for years.

I was attending a real-estate seminar one day when I began a conversation with a complete stranger. In relaying, that my purpose for attending was to learn the ins and outs of purchasing properties, I also mentioned how I'd come to this point.

To my surprise the stranger suggested that if I had managed to pull myself up from the previous failure that happened before I had relocated, then why not market that knowledge to others.

I thought it was a terrible idea, but we had exchanged phone numbers, and each time we spoke thereafter, he'd bring up the idea again. In an effort to get him off my back, so to speak, I agreed to give it a try for couple of months.

I thought it would never work. I thought I was the only person who could possibly have things so screwed up. But since I had told him I would at least give it a try, I printed a few flyers and posted them around my neighborhood. To my utter amazement, it didn't take long before I was taking on clients, and once again rebounding from a whether dark place.

I found there were many people experiencing what I had experienced. I took the knowledge that I had, formed a credit and financial services business, that I later coined and named CREDITDEFENDER^{SM}. A combination of two words I combined that not only told the public exactly what I did, but later would become popular in some varying degrees with others who would also attempt to profit by the term. Yes, if you have ever heard the name, I am the man that originated the term.

That business would go nationwide, and at last put me in the position to manage and control my own life. Through that business, I would counsel people from all walks of life including neighbors, professional athletes, entertainers, business owners, and more.

Because of my serious setbacks or failures, my rewards were greater than I thought they would ever be, and came from a place I never expected.

My point here is to stress, that the path to your dream may not always be the one you expect. But you can overcome any obstacle or so called failure once you are determined to succeed in your goal. When the universe sees that you are so focused and determined to live life on your terms, it has no choice but to supply the means by which you are able to do the thing you want to do.

I am very happy to say that after leaving that second job, I have never worked for anyone else other than myself. I am not trying to encourage you to do what I did. What I am encouraging you to do is to follow your own path. And if in following that path, you need guidance on just how to do it, I want to help by sharing the thought process that I not ony used, but countless of others that came before and after me have also used to achieve their goals.

Actually it took many years before I finally realized that my setbacks or failures are only setups for even greater success.

CHAPTER 7
PROCESS OF ELIMINATION

THAT'S WHAT I WANT YOU TO REALIZE. I want you to start rethinking your setbacks or failures. I believe if you can learn to reprocess your thoughts, you can possibly avoid years of living in mediocrity. You can improve your overall health, and financial circumstances. You can release yourself from artificial stimulates such as drugs, whether prescription or otherwise, alcohol, over eating, over spending, or any of the avenues you may be commonly using to mask the pain of not living out your dreams.

Your dream is yours, no matter how big or small others may view it. You have an inherit right to live it. But no matter the size or the nature of your dream, you will have to pay a price. You should not only expect, but also strategically analyze and learn from your failures, otherwise, you will never live the life you are capable of achieving.

I must stress, when saying "analyze" your failures, that does not mean that you take a long term or permanent vacation there. You simply stay calm, remain focused on your ultimate goal, and find out what pitfalls or errors you have made. By process of elimination, once you figure out what did not work, or what you don't want, you automatically shorten the list that leads to an outcome that will work, and leads to what you do want.

Sounds simple doesn't it? But surprisingly the simplest things in life can be the most difficult for us practice. That's exactly why I am here. I will help guide you through a process that will become your life time companion, and your friend. You will discover that the only motivation you will ever need is the ability to motivate yourself!

CHAPTER 8
STRATEGIC PLANNING

Contrary to what we may want to believe, the victory is not always given to the swiftest, the smartest, the strongest, most talented, best looking, or any of the many pronouns we might attach to a person of success. More often then not, the victory is given to some ordinary person just like you and I. It is given to the person who first holds a constant vision in his or her mind, and cannot accept, will not accept that the vision can't become their reality.

Think of it as if you were planning a road trip from your home right now, to someplace, let's say a thousand miles away. Your thought process automatically envisions the desired outcome even before you begin the journey. And because it is something you are looking forward to, you are motivated not by outside sources, but by your own will power to ensure you enjoy the highlights that will benefit your experience. In preparation, and since it is a "road trip," you will most likely, make sure your vehicle is in somewhat dependable condition, plan a few stops along the way, decide on some place to stay, maybe select some eateries, some sites to see, and whatever would make your trip pleasant, exciting, and memorable to you. You would plan some type of budget to get you there and back.

In short, you have set a goal. Now in the planning, although you hope everything goes smoothly, you also allow for some adjustments. Some unforeseen events or complications, that might possibly happen. You don't focus on these events, nor do you allow them to deter you from getting in your vehicle and starting the journey.

But as we have all heard, if not experienced, there are times when even the most carefully laid plans can go awry. Let's say you get several hundred miles into the journey and something totally unexpected and completely super challenging arises, what would you do?

You only have three options, you can turn around and go back, you can stay where you are, or you can find a way to reach your destination. That's the way everything in life is, you only have what seems to be, three choices.

However, in essence, as we all know, since everything is in constant change, if you choose to stay where you are, you have in a sense given up or digressed into a state likely worst than before you started the journey. So then, in reality you must either go backwards or you must continue forward.

If you can take this same analogy and apply it across the board of your life, you will see that although there are many things you can not control, the one thing you can control is how you will react.

Let's take a look at the example of Malala Yousafzai. Here is a very normal and seemly everyday person who had a goal. Her goal although to some seemed a natural part of life, in her environment was by some powerful forces considered, unnatural. That goal was simply to get an education in a society that made it difficult simply because of her gender.

That goal, that vision led her into an extreme circumstance. By all accounts, it appeared to some that she had failed. However, in her mind, in her vision, she used what was suppose to be her failure or the end of her dream, not only to propel her forward, but to reach and inspire millions with her determination not only to achieve her goal, but also take an active part in standing up for the education of others, especially the education of women and children in her native home.

By using what was meant to be her failure as a milestone to bring her closer to her goal, she has gone much farther and achieved much more than she even may have envisioned at the outset. That simple goal by an ordinary person, has made giant waves in the sea of humanity.

Not only do you have this same ability, you also have the same opportunity. The ability, and the opportunity to carry out your vision. You were supplied with this ability at birth. And because you were supplied with the ability, the universe has automatically prepared the opportunities you will need in order to achieve the goal.

CHAPTER 9
MAKING THE GRADE

REMEMBER OUR THEORY of thinking of the universe as a classroom. Because the size of your opportunities must match the goal, then the universe makes the size of your challenges, or obstacles equal to those opportunities. As you gain knowledge and skills, you then are expected to accept the greater and more difficult challenge of moving to the next level or grade. You don't concern yourself as much about all the individual test scores received on pop quizzes, and test you take during the year, as you do about the grade on your final exam.

That's the way life is, don't be so concerned if sometimes you miss the mark, you have a setback, or you don't know the answer. Instead analyze how the event will play out over the long term of your life, and what effect it will have in your life's journey. In many cases you will find you are giving to much weight to things that have little effect, and giving not enough weight to things that have great effect.

In other words, because you are spending so much energy and time sweating the small stuff, you are depleting yourself of the energy and focus you need in order to pursue the things that are truly most important to you. And because time stands still for no one, you may now find yourself to overwhelmed to hold to your dreams.

I say, if you are still reading this book, or listening to it's audio, then although you may seem overwhelmed, I'm confident that I can help revitalize your drive if you are willing to accept and make a few basic changes in your life.

No matter where you are mentally, physically, or spiritually, the universe has already prepared everything that you need in order to live the life you desire. It has already set the conditions that are needed for you to reach your destination regardless of your past or present circumstance.

Nature is not so cruel as to give us an inherit desire and then not supply all that is needed in order, to obtain that desire. The cruelty is in ourselves because we make excuses such as age, economic background, race, gender, social status, or whatever suits our agenda so that we don't have to admit we are just afraid of failure.

Don't kid yourself, if you knew with a given guarantee that your goals would be met, ask yourself how many things you would reach for? Would it be a better career, a larger home, a different mate, or maybe just a better you? Stop for a moment, get a pen, and write your own desires here:

_____
_____
_____
_____.

Do not be concerned how out of reach these desires may seem, or that someone else might see them. In fact, one of the probable reasons you are not getting what you desire is because you have not only neglected to write down your goals, but you've also been afraid to express them to others simply because you fear what they might say or think.

Now ask yourself why you are not working towards these means. In all likelihood, when you dismiss all your excuses, the bottom line is nothing more than your fear of failure.

CHAPTER 10
CURING MENTAL ROADBLOCKS

Because you are innately this creations preeminent being, did you know that fear of failure is actually from your own manufacturing or imagination?

Nature has only provided us with two inborn fears, the fear of falling and the fear of loud noises. All others are pretty much built by our own perception, and the mindset we choose to perceive and give power to.

Therefore fear of failure is something you choose and not something imposed upon you by some cruel act of fate. In fact, it actually goes against your true character. So it is no wonder that it therefore causes unwanted side effects when you allow it to infiltrate your being. Naturally, for the sake of survival there are circumstances in which your fears can be of great value, however, in the course of your every day existence this is usually not the case.

The fact is you've become so complacent with the fear of failure that in most cases you don't even recognize that the infection has taken hold. So much so that when an occasion arises that brings a certain desire to the surface, you will automatically allow the infection to reason out why things are just better left as they are.

In medicine one of the ways to fight an infection is sometimes to inject the person with a strain of the live virus. While this may seem odd, what it often does is to help build up your immune system so that your body can actually resist the more serious illness associated with the virus.

Let's think of failures in the same way. Instead of allowing them to be a costly or deadly disease, let us think of them as small injections that prevent us from making more costly mistakes so that we can move closer to our goals. The same way the tiny sting of an injection can build up your immunity to disease, you should allow the sting of your failures to build up your tolerance to nay sayers, and yourself when it comes to living your own desired life style.

I will not lie to you, because what I want is for you to be honest with yourself. This new and different way of thinking although quite simple, is not that easy. I know we all want instant gratification, and painless ways of doing things. But to sugar coat your importance in making this change would be unfair. Therefore if you are not willing to put in the work that I am and will be suggesting, you will not be able to move beyond your present state of existence.

It took time, perhaps many number of years for you to settle into the mindset that you now have. You have become comfortably seared in your way of thinking. There will be no magic pill, no magic solution that can undo what is perhaps a lifetime of damage in just a day's worth of reading, a day in some motivational seminar, or even a few week's worth of halfhearted attempts.

But if you are consistent and determined enough, change will take effect. And only you and you alone can put in the sweat equity to do the work. Just as in physical exercise, where there is no pain, there can be no gain.

Only if you are willing to devote time and effort each day to focusing on retraining your thought process will these procedures work. As you continually practice counteracting negative and non productive thinking with thoughts of what you perceive to be abundance, like the out of shape person who starts and maintains a workout routine, you will gradually begin to experience changes that are reflected by the intensity of your efforts.

As quoted by James Allen, "You cannot travel within and stand still without." The question here is, where is your mind traveling to? Is it continually moving in the direction of lack, unhappiness, hardship, disappointment, or is it continually moving in the direction of abundance, happiness, freedom, excitement and success?

We so often think we will feel better when things get better, which is completely backwards. Successful people have discovered that things actually get better when we think better, which causes us to feel better. So the key is to constantly take any situation and through your thought process, control it whether than allowing it to control you.

CHAPTER 11
ART OF THE SELF SELL

NATURE AND THE UNIVERSE displays many awe inspiring wonders, but no matter how great or how small, everything must face resistance. And in facing the resistance only the animal, plant, or mineral that can withstand and benefit from the resistance, will survive.

There is no such thing as an "easy" life. Everything in existence has to fight, has to compete, has to work to survive be it animal, plant, or mineral. Yes, even the lowly mineral has to face resistance in order to shine. Some of our most precious gems come from metamorphic rocks and minerals that under high heat and pressure, transform into jades, emeralds, opals, tourmalines and diamonds. Yes, even the precious diamond is formed only after a lowly lump of coal is superheated and put under intense pressure.

The only difference between any of these and you, is that you, have been given the gift of choice. You are not constrained to accepting a predetermined plight. You can not always choose or change the circumstances, but you can always choose or change the outcome, simply by how you react. So instead of thinking that your failures are proof that you are merely a lowly lump of coal, you should view them as opportunities to make you stronger until you are shining brightly like the diamond you are meant to be.

Though like many diamonds, you may be flawed, you should not focus on the flaws but focus instead on your brilliance. When you begin to focus on your talents, and your abilities despite what others might say or think, it will only be a matter of time before they also begin to see your beauty. They to will begin to notice just how brightly you shine. You will eventually begin to shine so brightly that they will not even notice the flaws. All they will notice is the positive impact you are having on the lives of those around you. They themselves will also begin to become supporters of your cause simply because you are showing leadership in every facet of your life.

We are living at a time in history when more than ever, it is vital that you learn to master your own values, ideas, and opinions.

Today's society is constantly being bombarded by what other's want us to believe. More often than not, outside influence happens because others are attempting to sell us some product or service. They want us to believe that we must have the latest new gadget, drive the latest car, wear the most stylist fashion, taste the newest food craze, or whatever they are selling.

Your mind is continually being blasted with these images. And why, because these advertisers know it is worth thousands, sometimes billions of dollars to plant an image in your brain, and then to feed you that image until you are so convinced that the product or service is needed, that you actually buy into it.

They understand that if you hear or see something often enough, you will then feel you need or want it as a part of your existence. Have you ever heard a song or jingle that you really disliked or cared very little for, and it was played over, and over again on the radio or TV? Did you at some point find that even when you were away from those media, the tune kept repeating in your brain? Did you also notice that as it kept repeating, you gradually came to actually accept and enjoy it?

Well if that is true, why not program your own personal saying, that fits your needs, your desires, your goals, and start repeating it over and over to yourself. You don't have to reinvent the wheel, just apply or copy what has already been proven to work for these multi-billion dollar companies. Like the tune you originally didn't like or care for, your personal saying will eventually become quite natural. You will then find a means to bring it into reality just as you did that new car, that latest phone, entertainment center, or whatever it was you allowed repeated ads to sell you. You will begin to see youself progressing forward, and will be inspired to continue along your chosen journey.

Create your own personal ad to first sell yourself. Tell yourself repeatedly that you are confident, you are healthy, you are strong, you are creative, you are prosperous, or whatever ad you want to create for yourself. If you are committed to replaying it over and over again in your mind, like the song you once disliked, it will eventually, become comfortable. It will be so comfortable in fact that once you have truly solidified it in your thought process, it will start to manifest in your actions. This goes back to the concept "you cannot travel within and stand still without."

After all, isn't that the reason McDonald's sells so many hamburgers, Apple sells so many phones, Ford sells so many vehicles, and other successful businesses continually seem to flourish? They solidify it in our minds that the product or service is great. Once solidified, we then find the means by which to obtain what they are offering simply because we now desire that brand or product.

Now don't get me wrong, I totally believe in and support free enterprises. My point here is if they have figured out that planting a repeated image or audio loop in our minds brings them positive results, why not take that same technique and transform yourself into who you desire to be by using those same methods in which to formulate your own self persuasive ad.

You have plenty of examples of successful people, products, and services that you can learn from. The only thing that needs reinventing is your way of thinking.

This is why I am committed to helping those and only those who sincerely desire to be helped.

There tons of self-help books, motivational speakers, clergy persons, and professional leaders that promote positive thinking. Masses of people attend seminars, workshops, and religious or spiritual events to get them excited about life. The problem is the majority can only maintain that euphoric feeling for a limited amount of time before they fall back into old habits, and old ways of thinking.

But if you are one of the few who truly want change, no matter how minor or drastic, then I can help you transform your life by simply guiding you through procedures that will remain with you long after you have read this book.

You will take with you something you may have given up or never knew you had. You will take power, you will take control, and you will take responsibility for your own destiny.

CHAPTER 12
TRASH CAN BECOME YOUR TREASURE

NOW LET'S REMEMBER, we are starting by rethinking the word "failure," so let's look at another example where failure was used as milestone to built a great success. Just about everyone is familiar with the Post-it® notes. But did you know that they were created as a result of a failed operation?

You see, the 3M company was attempting to formulate a strong adhesive. Unfortunately, the man that developed the adhesive found that his invention was actually weaker than what the company already had. To all appearances, the new adhesive was a failure, and no one knew quite what to do with it. However, it's creator did not discard the formula. Several years later, another scientist for completely different reasons needed some adhesive and remembered the glue that had been set aside and considered as useless or a failure. He decided to try the formula for a different purpose. Yes, you guessed it, he applied the formula to pieces of plan paper, and voila, to his amazement it worked without damaging anything. And that my friends is the birth of the ever popular Post-it® notes.

Because he looked a the failed product, from a crisp and new perspective, he was able to use that failure as a milestone that would lead to one of the simplest, and yet most widely used products in the world.

So, I have not only suggested that you start retraining your thought process, but I have given you a number of very ordinary and commonly known scenarios that support what I am telling you. Now that you have a small glimpse of just how you have been effected by your thinking, you can probably think of many other examples on your own.

You can probably actually list more events where this has been the case than you previously imagined or have given serious thought to. We've heard the mottoes such as "one man's trash is another man's treasure," "if at first you don't succeed, try, try again," and one that I particularly like is from Robin Robert's mother, Lucimarian Tolliver, "make your mess your message."

So obviously, this is not some hidden secret, nor is it some new or strange idea. Why then is it so hard for the majority of people to grasp what is apparently crystal clear?

Is it because we can't "see the forest for the trees?" In other words are we so caught up, so focused on the circumstances that are surrounding us that we fail to realize there is a very scenic path that has already been trodden, and all we really have to do is stay on and follow that path.

No one has all the answers, and no one can do a thing alone. Whoever you are and whatever you desire to do or become, more likely than not, someone has traveled that path or one similar to it before.

You need others to support your efforts, but you can't do that if you have your own misgivings about what you are trying to promote. And since what you are trying to promote is yourself, you must become your number one fan.

Not in an egotistical way, but in a way that says you will not buckle under pressure. In a way that respects others and their point of view, while at the same time maintaining your divine individuality, your divine inheritance, your divine rights as a human that is put here to embrace and experience the wonders of life.

At the end of the day, the end of your journey, the end of your life, do you really want to leave feeling that someone or something has robbed you of savoring the desires that you have in your heart?

If that should happen, there is no one to blame but self. People may rob you of physical possessions, circumstances may rob you of some specific opportunity. But there is no one, nor is there any circumstance that can rob you of your dream.

Therefore, since possessions can be replaced, and circumstances can change, if you are robbed it is only because you have robbed yourself.

Everyone wants to live and have an abundant life, but few are willing to do the work. We want to get it by winning the lottery, going to the casino, marrying into it, winning the sweepstakes. Anything other than putting ourselves out there and claiming what the universe says is rightly ours.

And even if you are one of the few lucky

people that is destined to inherit a windfall, it will not change your emotional state of being. There are numerous people who have more material wealth than they will ever need who are just as poor in spirit as someone that is homeless and living under a bridge.

I've had the opportunity to work with some people that our society has in every way considered to be the most successful, brightest, and creative. Yet some were more unhappier, and yes, in deeper debt than you might imagine.

And although by most definitions they are successful, the bottom line is they to have suffered from the same fear of failure. You see your success or failure is not dependent on the size of your home, the make of your vehicle, or the size of your bank account.

What it is dependent upon is your state of being. People who have material possessions still face obstacles such as health issues, family crisis, critics, and all the trappings that go into everyday life. They are no different in the sense that we all have twenty-four hours each day. We all must eat, sleep, use the restroom, bathe, pay taxes, and do the things that can sometimes seem quite mundane. They have the same feelings and emotions as anyone else. Therefore, the only thing that makes the truly successful person any different from the commoner is their way of thinking.

No matter what your economic status, gender, race, or religious believe, you must always see yourself as a winner. You must remove the word failure completely from anything in your mind that associates the word with you.

The first thing you should do when you rise to greet the day, is to give thanks that you have successfully awaken to experience, and take in the breath of life. Then you should command your day by speaking the things you want to accomplish, and how you expect them to play out.

For example, you might tell yourself something like, "I am thankful for awaking and finding that I am safe. I expect this to be a wonderful day as I work on the task of advancing in my career. The actions I take today are bringing me future security."

Then the last thing you do again at night, is give thanks that you have journeyed through another day, and express eagerness to experience what the next day will bring.

In that eagerness, and that expectation, you must refuse to allow anything other than positive outcomes to be an option. You must make it clear, that even if it doesn't turn out the way you would like, there will still be something good gained from the experience. Even if that something is nothing more than allowing you to eliminate that option and/or situation, and approach it from another angle.

This is important because events have to be planned. They seldom just happen. Isn't it true that in most cases you plan what you want to eat, you plan where you want live, you plan what you want to drive, or wear, or buy. Without realizing it, you are in a constant state of planning. Planning is so natural that you don't even realize that you are constantly planning. So then why not plan your destiny in the same way.

Since the idea may be new to you, it might and should feel a bit uncomfortable at first, but eventually just as the many other things you plan so naturally that make you who you are, and define your personality, this to will become equally as natural as you evolve into the person you truly desire to be.

What makes you think that you will feel better, become braver, and be happier when your circumstances change? This is a major disillusion. The fact is your circumstances will only change, when you feel better, become braver, and live happier.

If you feel good about yourself, you are in a much better position to be assertive and step into the unknown simply because you are more confident. And if you stop complaining and embrace happiness right where you are, you will be excited about life. That excitement will breed energy, and that energy will bring about different circumstances.

These actions will allow you to let go of relationships, addictions, disparaging habits, and other things that are not in accordance with the person you are evolving into. You will then find you haven't lost anything at all. These voids will now be filled with stronger and kinder relationships, uplifting interest, encouraging habits, and only things that are in accordance with your dreams simply because you have refused to leave room for anything else.

Right within the word "fail" itself, is the word "ail." We all know what an ailment is. It's a physical or emotional pain, discomfort, or trouble. Also closely related is the word "frail," which means weak, breakable, delicate, fragile.

Is this really how you want to think of yourself? Don't you respect yourself enough to detach from such definitions? What is your value? Are you going to allow someone or something else to decide, or make that final decision for you? Don't be deceived, if you don't define your worth, others will do it for you, and you can be sure it will always be less than what it should be.

However, when you take a stand, when you step from the shadows and define your own worth, you will be surprised just how many people will actually agree and support you.

It doesn't mean you have to be inconsiderate or unkind to others, quite the contrary. Because you feel free, you feel successful, you feel happy, you will automatically radiate the same joy to others. You will want them to experience the same exhilaration.

That is one of greatest beauties of re-thinking failure. Just as misery loves company, people that are happy want to be surrounded by others who are happy.

If you are afraid of failure, take a look at the people you socialize with. Without even personally knowing you, I can feel quite comfortable in saying that your associates are people who like you share the same fear. Your associates are like a mirror. Look into that mirror as well as looking into yourself. If you don't like what you see in the mirror, the only way to change it is to change yourself.

It all begins and it ends with you. You must take a brutal, but honest assessment of yourself. This is the reason most self-help books, tapes, seminars, and yes even some coaches fall short of helping those in need. It isn't so much that the programs or coaches themselves are flawed, as it is in the student or the client. All is fine as long as the general audience is targeted, but when you become the "bull's eye" of that target so to speak, can you face what is factual about your own shortcomings?

I have witnessed this a number of times with

people who have sought out my help, when all they really wanted was someone who agreed with them, or to confirm they had every reason to feel as they did.

How many times has a friend, family member, or co-worker came to seek your advice on any given matter? Did you find after you'd given them an alternate solution, they responded back with all the reasons why your suggestions could not be applied to their situation? Or maybe they just didn't respond back at all, giving you a blank look that's says "you just don't fully understand the situation at hand."

Are you doing the exact same thing? Do you and your acquaintances use one another as sounding boards to express your agonies without ever really embracing the solutions that might be coming from such encounters? Remember, your closest associates are people you have lots in common with. That's why I say your friends are like a mirror. If you see that trait in them, you more than likely are a victim of that same trait.

Until you make a very conscience decision to not just alter, but completely get rid of that trait, there will be no help for you.

This may not be what you want to hear, but I will not apologize for giving you the tools you really need to move forward from where you are. I am committed to your cause, but you are and must be your greatest ambassador.

I will support you, hold you up, and cheer you on. I will not carry you. I believe in the adage, "Give a man a fish, and you feed him for a day. Teach a man to fish, and you feed him for a lifetime."

That's why I am here, to supply the tools you yourself need in order to get the best results from any given situation, even if that situation is what the average person might consider to be a failure.

Do you really want to be average? I don't believe you do. It's against nature. No matter who you are, and what you want from life, you want it to be the best that you determine yourself to be. And not what society, or any one else decides is acceptable and imposes upon you.

Consider this, if you are currently in pain and suffering a life that you are not finding enjoyment with, than why not instead suffer the pain that will eventually lead to the life you want? The first type of pain, which is your current status can only be permanent. However, the second type of pain is temporal because it will get you where you want to go.

All I can do is point out your options, only you can make the final choice. Will you be the victim or will you be invincible, unbeatable, unconquerable, unstoppable, and victorious?

I believe you can, now I want you to believe it to!

If you don't take the first steps to start your journey, you will never reach your destination. Every step taken shortens the distance. So no matter how small or how large a step you take, commit to moving forward.

Do something every day that is specifically targeted towards any achievement you want to accomplish. Don't worry if some days you find yourself feeling a little less energetic, a little less enthusiastic. That's just called being human.

There will be times, especially in the beginning when you will feel less inspired simply because your mind has been conditioned into believing the story you have told yourself up to this point. Like a less superior being than you are, you have trained yourself to respond to certain stimuli. If your response has been less than satisfying, the only way to change your plight, is to change the focus of your mind's inner eye. Why is this so important, because each day that passes means that you are closer to living your dream than you have every been.

When properly used, resistance is a wonderful tool. Resistance can build strength, it can build confidence, it can build character. It is not so important that you are on fire with energy every day as it is that you are consistent with some action regardless of how great or small that action may be each day.

Once you are consistent in changing your habitual way of thinking, you will eventually find yourself more energetic, and more enthusiastic simply because you actually not only feel yourself, but also see yourself getting closer to your goal.

You will experience the victory of smaller milestones along the way. Eventually, you will acquire so many of these smaller victories that you feel there is no way you can possibly be comfortable going back from whence you came.

It's sort of like if you decided to swim across the ocean. Before you even begin, you already know the quest will not be easy. You don't expect it to be easy. You don't even want it to be easy, which is the very reason you've chosen the challenge.

You take your first steps into the salty waters of the sea and for the first few yards, it's not so hard. As you get farther and farther out, the waters get deeper and deeper. Eventually it's so deep that's it's over your head, and you must begin to swim. And although you can't yet see it, the opposite shoreline is just a little closer.

As you continue to swim farther and farther out, your body begins to get tired, you begin to feel less inspired. You reach a point where your brain tells you to go back. But if you resist, if you keep moving forward there will come a point that even when your mind tells you to go back, your spirit will reason that you have come to far, and you will get bursts of energy that will keep you swimming ahead.

If you can obey your spirit and continue, there will then come a point when although your body says to go back, your mind will then reason that you are now closer to the other side than you are from the starting point. What will happen then, is because both your mind and your spirit are in sync they will over ride any reasoning that your body may be expressing.

Because your mind and spirit are stronger, they will force your physical body to do what is necessary in order to complete the task.

You should not take this lightly. Your mind and your spirit governs your body. Therefore, if you want your body to experience any sensation, whatever it be, you must learn to utilize the mastery of first feeling it in your spirit and in your mind.

We spend so much energy and time working on our exterior. We are often like neatly wrapped packages, with pretty bows and ribbons on the outside, but inside we are hollow, we are jaded, we are not at all what we appear to be.

We concern ourselves with what others think of us, when we don't even think much of ourselves. Oh sure, we say we do, but if we did would we really care if we rocked the boat, stepped away from the crowd, and did the unexpected?

Why do you live where you live, dress as you do, work where you work, drive what you drive? Is it because these things really express who you are, or do they just express who you want others to believe that you are?

Are you afraid to be different, or to be original? Do you put yourself in debt mentally, physically, spiritually, as well as financially just because you want to keep up with others? Why can't you say, no? Why can't you choose to make some smaller sacrifices now so that you can reap even greater rewards later?

Who told you that you had to walk a certain path? Was it someone else, or was it you? Bottom line, it may have started out as someone else, but the blame lies squarely on your shoulders because you caved in. You are the one who told yourself these lies. You have repeated them in your mind so often, that you have hypnotized yourself into believing whatever trained inaction you have decided to take.

CHAPTER 13
THE EXPERIMENT

I ONCE HAD THE RARE OPPORTUNITY to conduct research at one of the country's leading universities, University of Rochester. I spent an entire summer working in their behavior lab. It was in that lab that we used animals such as primates, birds, mice, & rats to learn things about the thought and reasoning process of humans.

During my time there, I was given a pigeon that for no apparent reason, I named Pope. Anyway, I decided to see if I could train Pope to perform certain actions by rewarding him with treats.

I utilized a specialized cage to which I had an automatic feeder attached. When I first placed Pope in the cage, to him it was just like any other cage he was accustomed to. Therefore, to first get his attention, I would randomly, and periodically activate the feeder to drop some seed.

It didn't take long for that bird to associate the feeder with something he desired. In a short time, he came to the point where he'd just stand there expecting that at some point something would drop. And with patience without any action on his part, he would be rewarded.

That however was not my objective. What I wanted to do was teach him that he could control the feeder by performing certain acts. The first thing I taught him to do was distinguish when he had an opportunity to eat and when he didn't.

I had a button added to the feeder with a light inside. If the light was white, he could not get the treat. However, if I turned the light green, he without failure could expect his desired treat.

Because he had gotten accustomed, to just standing and patiently waiting, it took some coaxing, but it wasn't long before he realized he only got a treat when the light was green. At that point, I took it up a notch, I decided to only turn the light green if he pecked it three times. Again, with patience and some coaxing the bird, after a series of his own trial and error, or for the sake of our main topic, we'll call them trail and failure steps, came to realize he not only needed to wait for the light to turn green, but he also had to peck it three times, no more or no less, to make it turn green.

I was getting the bird to see, that he himself could satisfy his own desire if he were willing to do the work. He needed to not only adapt to his environment, but also determine his limitations, and adjust his actions by determining when and how he should respond. Once he'd reasoned that the feeder contained something he desired, and through sure determination, found the means by which to achieve it, I once again upped the ante. I'd gotten him to associate that he had to wait for the light to turn green, by pecking it three times, so I controlling his environment, decided he must now turn around 360 degrees in addition to the previous two steps. And he quickly through his trail and failure efforts, also figured that pattern out.

As a last and final test to prove that the bird not only understood, but also recognized his success or failure was based on his conditioning, I then placed a regular paper tablet on top of the cage. The goal here was to make Pope reason out that no matter what he did or how many times he did it, when the tablet was on top of the cage, he would not get that treat he so desired. It was also my way controlling how much the bird would consume, as I didn't want him to become overweight by continually consuming the treats.

Within approximately a ten week period of time , and working with the bird for about an hour or so each day, he'd adapted to everything I wanted him to do.

This is nothing new or secret, as you yourself have more likely than not heard of the experiment of Pavlov's Dogs.

Now if even animals can learn to adapt and retrain their thinking in such a way that will reward them with what they want, why do you think you are any different? We casually throw around the term "birdbrain," when the fact is you may have been manifesting those same symptoms without even realizing it.

You may have allowed someone or something outside of yourself to cause you to respond as they would have you respond. The good news is that unlike Pope, or Pavlov's dog's, you can decide to control when and what buttons are pushed. You can take back your control, instead being controlled.

If you have become nothing more than a human example of Pope or Pavlov's dogs, it's you that have allowed circumstances outside of yourself into conditioning you to act and react in ways that go against your nature.

Take back your control, even if your environment suggest that you cannot. That was what I wanted Pope to learn, that although he lived under certain rules, he still could control how, if, and when he wanted to respond.

The only real difference here is you as a human, unlike an animal, can control your environment. The answer is quite simple, if you don't like it, change it. Yes, it may be a bit uncomfortable, it may even require some huge sacrifices, but if it eventually leads you where you want to go, isn't it worth it?

Just as you control the external environment, of your home, car, or office, control the internal environment of your mind. Adjust your thoughts to bring you to the level of comfortability you not only desire, but also deserve.

And why do you deserve it? Because you are willing to do the necessary work. You want to feel worthy because you are worthy and not just because you think something should be handed to you. You want to be able to say you put in the work, you did the time, you paid in sweat equity. I guarantee, it will make you feel good when you look back over your journey and realize just what a magnificent work of art you have become.

CHAPTER 14
THE ENEMY WITHIN

SURE THERE ARE SOME who will read this book, and still choose to ignore that it's their fault if things are bleak. They will still blame someone or something else, and frankly I am not concerned with them. I am however concerned with you. Obviously, you want change, and all you need is someone helping you to see yourself objectively. You must be able to see yourself much clearer than you have ever seen yourself before. You must be able to admit that the person you are now is your enemy. This is not who you are meant to be. You must recognize this, and you must acknowledge this, if you are to transform your life.

Even if it comes from someone other than myself, you will have to at some point acknowledge that no one has let you down but yourself. You are not a child, therefore, you are expected to take care of yourself. That doesn't only mean when things are going well, but also, and more importantly when things are going wrong. The only two things you should expect in life, as they say, are death and taxes. All else must in some degree or another be earned.

No one owes you anything, nor should you owe anyone anything. We are all in this thing together. We help one another, we support one another, we inspire one another. If you are not doing that, then why should you expect or enjoy having an abundant life?

And just what is an abundant life? The answer will be different for everyone to some degree. However, no matter how you define it, it more than likely means security, happiness, good health, a level of prosperity, and respect for and from others. But you can only expect these benefits when you sow seeds that will produce these fruits.

You can not plant a cactus, and expect it to grow oranges. Likewise, you can not plant negative thoughts of despair, and expect life to manifest joy. Just as in nature, when you plant a seed, you expect it to yield a full crop. But that will only happen when and if you till the soil, fertilize the seed, and pull the weeds up by their roots. With the proper care and sunlight, one seed can multiply itself many times over. It can provide more than enough if and only if it is properly cared for.

That is same way your brain works. What ever you put into it, is what you will not only get back, but it will return magnified many times over. If you have fallen into a dark and seemly inescapable place in your life, it is only because you have allowed negative thoughts like weeds to infiltrate you mind.

The negative thoughts have become so

frequent and intense that whenever a positive thought, or good seed, so to speak, is planted it is choked out by the weeds. You have not left any room for the positive thought to really take root and mature so that it can produce anything good. You are so focused on weeds, that you don't notice the seedling that is even trying to sprout.

Therefore, because you don't see any good fruit being brought forth, you assume something is wrong with the soil, when in essence, the only thing wrong is that you are refusing to till the earth.

You have all the tools that you need, but they will do you no good if you never take the initiative to use them. You must also accept the fact that the more overgrown you have allowed these negative thoughts and actions to become, the more diligence it will require in order to shift the tide. That's really the issue here. Do you have the drive and the determination to do the things that must be done?

If someone told you to be at a specific location at a given time and they would give you brand new luxury vehicle of your choice, would you be there? In all likelihood, the answer is yes. And why, because it is something that you desire. Because you desire it so much, you wouldn't allow anything to prevent you from getting to the designated location. You would make it a priority. You would be there, and you would get your car. If you knew for a surety that you had the winning lottery numbers a week before the drawing, would anything keep you from purchasing a ticket?

You'd do these things because you'd make sure nothing impeded or stood in your way. We all would like things to be certainties in our lives. Wake up, that is not the way life is! It never has been, and it never will be. So unless you learn to change your way of thinking, and play life by it's rules, not the ones you want to imagine and conjure up your own mind, you will never be victorious.

CHAPTER 15
WRITING YOUR OWN SCRIPT

LET'S TAKE A QUICK LOOK behind two of today's most successful people.

J.K. Rowlings had been rejected numerous times before finding her success with the Harry Potter series. But how did she view or handle her failures? Here is what she had to say, "I was set free because my greatest fear had been realized and I still had a daughter that I adored, and I had an old typewriter and a big idea. And so rock bottom became a solid foundation on which I rebuilt my life."

Rock bottom, from there she build an empire by using her "big idea," or vision in addition to her failures to propel her forward. She used the word "rebuilt," which means she got rid of the old and started with something new. I would venture to say, the something new that she started with was nothing more than increased determination.

Spanx founder Sara Blakely was rejected on numerous occasions after spending time, investing money, and energy into developing and patenting her product. Nearly every major hosiery mills representative initially turned her away before she got her break.

It's obvious that she must have viewed these failures from a different perspective, that others woud have considered as sure signs to quit and give up. And because she looked at those failures from a different perspective, today her idea is a reality that both woman and even men can not live without.

These women like countless other people had absolutely no tangible guarantee that they would succeed. But they most definitely did have an intangible guarantee. That guarantee came not from outside sources, but from deep seated belief that they themselves had everything needed in order to achieve their dream despite what others may have thought.

The question is, where do you get that deep seated belief from? Are you born with it, or is something you must learn? And if you are born with it, can it learned by those who aren't lucky enough to be born with it?

I can't really answer whether or not a person

is born with that trait. Personally, I believe that some are, but I don't know for sure. What I do know for sure, is that it can be learned. Of that I have no doubt.

If you are struggling trying to find your way, the simplest thing to do is to emulate the actions that other's have used to find their place. Each person we have mentioned in this book started out just being everyday normal people. They were not born into royalty, or wealth. They came from various walks of life. They all had failures that could have prevented them from moving forward. But they also had the will within themselves to know their own worth, to set their own value, and to stay on coarse despite the magnitude of their setbacks or failures.

You don't need other's to give you what you already have. To some degree, you already have confidence. The problem is, you've allowed outside circumstances to make you doubt yourself. Since you have spent much time listening to opinions of others, you have forgotten how to trust your instincts. You are hearing and seeing with your physical ears and eyes, when you should be listening to your inner voice, and seeing with your inner eye.

Because outside influence has become so loud, what confidence you have is being drowned out. And each time you allow the outside noise to enter, your confidence level diminishes more and more.

Just as a play writer pens the script and the scenes that a character must follow, you must write the script and the scenes you want in your mind. You must then play it out in your daily life, and speak the lines as you desire them to manifest. Shakespeare obviously knew this when he wrote, "All the world's a stage, and all the men and women merely players; they have their exits and their entrances, and one man in his time plays many parts." You are responsible for your own casting, and the parts in which you will play.

First you must start your plot with a beginning, a middle, and an ending. You must take the responsibility of being the writer, producer, director, and choreographer of your story. You must decide if is to be a disaster, comedy, drama, survival, romance, or any combinations of outcomes you are looking for. Then you do the casting, and first person to cast is yourself. You are the star of the show. Therefore, the plot or storyline should ultimately center around you. Then you start selecting other characters that will be supporting your endeavor.

Since you are the lead character, are you portraying yourself to others as you would like them to truly see you? Are you setting the stage to assure the outcome that you desire? And in so doing, you must always understand and keep in mind, that your cast is important. Without them, there is no story to be told. So you treat them with the same respect and kindness that you yourself are demanding. Do not refuse them the opportunity to share in the spotlight.

In your casting, have you surrounded yourself by people who are believers, upbeat, cheerful, supportive, positive characters? If not, maybe you will not only need to rethink the way you've been casting yourself, but you also need to rethink the way you have been casting your players. Sometimes, you just have to let some people go, regardless of who they are. If they are toxic to your environment, you owe it to yourself to release them from your plot.

Again, I stress, you owe it to yourself. This is not cruel, unkind, nor unfeeling, unless you decide to make it so, which is not something I endorse. But if you are going to start rewriting the script for your life, you undoubtedly have at least a few people you will need to release from the setting you are currently putting into place.

Since you are now playing a new role, a new character, one that is confident, secure, happy, and fulfilled, you will want and need new cast members that fit into these supportive roles. You must begin surrounding yourself by people who are moving forward towards their own goals. They will understand your struggles, and be there to support you when you are feeling weak.

You will be able to share with them your challenges. Not as a way of complaining and griping, but as a way of understanding that they too share common thoughts and dreams and are willing to make the sacrifices necessary to make their lives as well as the lives of others better. By mutually sharing in your struggles, you begin to bounce ideas off one another that not only stimulate your creative juices, but also allow you to explore options you may not have otherwise considered.

CHAPTER 16
UPPING THE ANTE

YOU ARE TAKING ON A CHALLENGE, but in reality, the only person you should ever be competing against is yourself. You should constantly push yourself. It really matters very little what your family, friends, co-workers, competitors, and neighbors are doing. You are not here to compete against them, but to be the very best that you can be.

By constantly striving to improve yourself, you will automatically outpace others in your field of endeavor. By always competing against yourself, by nature you will cause others to also up their game. But if you keep your mind's eye focused on your own goals, you will find that you are in the leadership position. You will reach the finish line in whatever you are attempting to accomplish.

The most important thing you can do is reach for the thing that seems nearly impossible for you to do or attain, provided it is within your realm of desires. There is nothing wrong with healthy outside competition for fun and for sport. But when it comes to your personal well being, you need not prove anything to anyone other than yourself.

If you are to be successful, you can't wait until you have all the answers. You must be willing to forge into the unknown with the expectation that you will either learn what you need to know along the way, or you will be guided to others who will provide the answers you do not have.

When successful people decide to take on a venture, be it business or personal, they are not looking to be an expert in every phase of what they are doing. In today's society, it would be difficult if not impossible to grasp everything you will need to know in order for you to launch that new business or new career.

You would not only need to understand your product or service, but you would also need to comprehend such things as advertising, web design, social media, accounting, marketing, and many other aspects of what makes a successful business and/or career. This holds true whether you are looking to start a business, change your career, or just advance in your present career. Technology is moving so rapidly you cannot expect yourself to always fathom everything you need to know. You will need a network of people that you can turn to for support.

Likewise, in your personal life, since you should be constantly growing, the only thing you need to know for sure is who you are, and what you are willing to accept in life. Once you have established the answer to these questions, you can then move forward with confidence that any other qualities or traits you need to learn and develop will automatically come to you when and as they are needed. You will also draw people into your inner circle that will inspire you with bright ideas, and creative ways of enjoying the life you have dedicated yourself to.

To help you begin, I strongly suggest you take the time to carefully and honestly fill out your answers to the following questions, and as a first and beginning step, also commit to an action you will take each day to move you closer in that direction. Only list what you willing to do in order to make your desires a reality.

What is it that I want to achieve in my career?

_____

_____

_____

_____

I commit myself each day to do the following:

_____

_____

_____

_____

What would make life happier in my home?

_____

_____

_____

_____

I commit myself each day to do the following:

_____

_____

_____

What can I do to improve my health?

_____
_____
_____
_____

I commit myself each day to do the following:

_____
_____
_____
_____

How will I get in touch with my spiritual core?

_____
_____
_____
_____

I commit myself each day to do the following:

_____

___

___

___

Who will I allow or disallow into my life?

___

___

___

I commit myself each day to do the following:

___

___

___

What new thing am I willing learn?

___

___

___

I commit myself each day to do the following:

_____

_____

_____

_____

You should now have six targeted goals as well as six committed actions.

This is part of your new beginning. At the outset, it may feel a bit uncomfortable, but that's the way it should feel, otherwise you are not expecting enough of yourself. You are starting with the most basic part of learning to rethinking any failures that may have already happened, as well as the ones you will encounter along the way.

Just as in physical exercise, it usually takes several weeks of continued and repeated behavior before something can become a habit. Likewise, you should continue read over your responses each day until they are ingrained in your memory. Once that stage is reached, you are then well on the way to making the changes in life that you desire.

Along with the previous answers you gave for writing down your desires at the beginning of this book, and personal ad you created for yourself, you now have three very significant tools that you will need in order to begin traveling your road to success.

Because you also have these three written and documented tools, you will also be able to better focus on what things are most important. It is very possible that you will find some of the same if not similar objectives listed in your list of desires, the personal ad you created, and this third step of your journey.

If there are duplicate or closely related items, this is very important because it tells you something about where your subconscious mind has been trying to lead you. Because these desires are obviously something you are truly wanting, you should make them your main priority.

This is where your real work begins. As you review and start to analyze your lists, you will need to decide in what logical order you can arrange your actions in order to dedicate time every day of your life to moving in that direction.

You will have to prioritize your list so that the more important things are done first. In so doing, you will most likely find that these require more effort on your part. It will allow you to determine if what you have listed is really something you are willing to work towards, or if it is just wishful thinking on your part.

Because you are now beginning to really define yourself, you may need to go back and re-evaluate some of the things you listed. This is perfectly okay, as it is only helping to define just what you are willing to do in order to reach your level of comfortability and happiness.

CHAPTER 17
PERFECTING YOUR BALANCE

NOW BECAUSE YOU HAVE these fundamental tools, you are well on the way to rethinking failure. Along with these basics steps, and more that will come into play as you progress forward, you will begin to feel more calm, and think more clearly when situations arise that try to pull you back or hold you down.

This is not something that you are committing to for a day, a week, a month, or even a year. This is something you are committing to for the rest of your life.

Being human, you are allowed a day or two when maybe you aren't quite at full capacity. But that's it, no longer or you will find it harder and harder to get back on track. Similar to when you break your diet or workout routine, the longer you stay off coarse, the more difficult it is to start again. Remember as I stated earlier in the book, it's not as important that you be on fire every day, as it is to do something consistently every day.

It's like the tortoise and the hare, better to constantly keep things moving forward, than to start strong and stop to take a rest.

By coming this far into the book, you have already begin the very first steps that can reshape your life. You will become stronger, and more creative with each passing day. There will eventually be a point when you will not even recognize the person that you are today.

For you there will be no such thing as failure or surrender. You will go places, and do things that you only thought about in your mind. They will become your reality. They will define the new you.

Remember, it is up to you to define your dreams. They may or may not require material wealth, but they will most definitely require spiritual wealth. That's the wealth that will keep you going through difficult times.

Tyler Perry is a perfect example of what spiritual wealth can do. He escaped an abusive household in order to pursue his dreams. As a result of making such a drastic choice, he ended up living in his car. Because of the spiritual wealth he had, he however was able view his failures from a completely different perspective. He lived through this situation and rebounded in a big way. A great rags-to-riches story.

Again, I am not suggesting that you emulate anyone I mention in this book, except to the degree that is helps you find your own individuality. Your desires should be personal, but you can learn from these leaders that have come from various walks of life. No matter what walk of life you choose to take, these principals, and these laws apply.

Everyone is not meant to be a millionaire or a billionaire. Everyone is not meant to be famous or well known. But everyone is meant to happy in their own right. There are those who have found their complete calling in life, and yet material things seem to matter very little to them. Nor do they seek to be famous or well known. They are people just like you and I. Important people in our communities. Teachers, policemen, firefighters, volunteers, neighbors, and friends. People we often undervalue, take for granted, and overlook who are the true heroes and sheroes of society. You must understand that real wealth can be had regardless of anything you might physically associate with it.

Therefore it is imperative that you search your inner being. This journey of rethinking your failures involves physical, mental, and spiritual activity. Physically, you must keep yourself as healthy as you can so that your body will be able to endure. If you know you are not eating a healthy diet, or getting enough rest and exercise, you must commit to make some changes. Your body needs nutritious and healthy fruits and vegetables if you are to optimize your energy level. You also need time to rest and relax, breaking away from routines that drain your energy. Mentally, you must constantly exercise your brain with new, creative, and positive thoughts. Instead of watching mindless TV, take some time to watch educational programming, inspiring movies based on true lives. Limit how much time you spend watching negative images on TV whether those images are Hollywood produced, or current events that happen and are shown repeatly via the news media each day. You are attempting to fill your brain with good images, so you must filter what is going into it. Spiritually, no matter what you believe, you must accept that universe is working by it's own laws, and if you don't understand, or follow these laws you will not be happy or successful. So take time each day to completely tune out the world, and get in touch with your spiritual being. Turn off the TV, any and all audio devices, and just enjoy the silence. You may be surprised to find what your spirit will reveal in only five or ten minutes. No matter who you are or what you believe, you know you are spirit, soul, and body. You must have balance in these areas of your life. Don't neglect being in touch with all three.

When you realign yourself in these three

major areas of life, there is absolutely no way you will ever again live depressed, feeling hopeless, or worthless. This is not a promise that your life will not have moments of bleakness, but that's what they will be. Moments that rarely creep in to try and destroy what you have built. But you will have gained the knowledge and skills to defeat them. They once had the power and the skills to overshadow any positive thoughts that tried to enter your brain, but you will learn to reverse the tide on them, so to speak and cast them out like the garbage they truly are.

CHAPTER 18
ENJOYING THE VICTORY

As you move forward along this journey of self-awareness, you begin to see life more clearly. You will discover the awesomeness that can only be understood by others who are on the same journey. It will become your duty as a recipient of these treasures to share what you have learned with those still seeking, but yet still lost, the experiences and the secrets that have led you to where you are. You will want them to discover within themselves the same powers that you have discovered.

As you encourage others, others will encourage you. There will be an endless supply of energy generated from within, as well as universal energy rushing forth to greet you because it knows you are on a mission. No longer will you feel rundown, uninspired, and incapable of taking on the challenges that will come your way.

Just as you have needed someone to share their zest for life with you, and help you discover the path that has always been there, but had been overgrown with the weeds of negative thoughts, you will begin helping others. When you feel complete and fulfilled, it allows you to give to others.

This is a duty, a calling to everyone that finds the path. You can do this because you realize you will never lack anything. There are enough resources in this world for everyone, with plenty more to spare. And the more good you do, the more abundantly good will return unto you. You will always have more than enough love, compassion, joy, peace, and unimaginable treasures to share. You will find that at long last you are living the abundant life. The life you wanted. The life you were willing to custom build.

Just like moving from a track home into one specifically designed for and by you, you will relish in your individuality. You will no longer live life by what others may consider to be the "norm", but you'll be back to the place that you originally considered to be your "norm." Back to your creativity and the true purpose of your existence.

CHAPTER 19
EPILOGUE

THIS IS NOW THE FIRST DAY of the rest of your life. Start where you are. The past cannot be changed, nor is your tomorrow guaranteed. This moment is the only time you have, so invest in it wisely. Regardless of what has happened to you in the past, refuse allowing yourself to go back there. There is no value in trying to rethink the past, but there is immeasurable value in rethinking the present.

You are blessed to be living in this space of time. The word "present," which is the age in which we live, implies something wonderful. It implies a gift, and that gift is free to everyone who will accept it. There is no need to hunger for answers, when you have resources at your finger tips that men have never had before.

You want information, search the internet. Any subject you can imagine is there. You need an emotional and or spiritual uplift, watch something positive on TV or on-line. Don't allow dark moments to stay with you. Do something, take a walk in the park, sit and listen to the sound of water rippling on the lake. Do anything but allow yourself to digress once you have begin this journey.

As I stated upfront, my object is to not only make your rethink your failures or setbacks, but more importantly, you must realize that the only real motivation you will ever need, is the ability to motivate yourself. You may think the tools you have received from reading this book are very basic. And they are. However that doesn't mean that they are not powerful. They are so powerful in fact that once you start applying them with consistency, you will find yourself moving mountains that you have never moved before.

As you move these mountains, you will gain knowledge and skills to add to these basics. Your conversations will change. No longer will you allow negative or disparaging chatter to consume your day. Instead, you will use your talents and your knowledge to recognize it for what it is. You will defeat it by standing tall and accepting that you are more than able to overcome any obstacle that may try to prevent you from enjoying the freedom you have now discovered.

You will never find yourself alone when you open your mind to the possibilities right within yourself. In your progression forward, along with myself, others are going to be here to help you. Other's who have traveled the path. We can help guide you, and in time, you will begin guiding others. Together we will make our marks on the world just by the people we have truly touched.

Now that you are beginning to realize that you cannot fail, you can only learn from unwanted outcomes and or circumstances, doesn't it feel better?

Isn't this what you have been wanting? Someone or something that could make a real difference in your life? Isn't it even more powerful and wonderful to learn, that that someone is you?

You can choose to ignore the principles that I have presented, but without them, you will never find your peace. Even if you should decide not to journey forward, you can never again comfortably place blame on anyone other than yourself.

These are not my standards, nor are they my laws. They belong to no one. They belong to the universe, and are enforced without prejudice of any nature on all mankind. And just as in the civil or penal laws, there are consequences to those who don't obey these laws, there are also consequences for those who don't obey the universal laws. The only real difference is you may from time to time, escape man's law, but rest assured, you will never escape universal law.

Since "the only thing that is constant, is change," you are either always progressing forward or you are digressing back. You are never really in the same position at any given time. You are different today than you where yesterday, and you will be different tomorrow than you are today. So since you are never the same at any given time, choose this as your time to always be progressing forward. Forward towards your dreams, your happiness, your stability, and your peace of mind as well as your peace in spirit.

No matter what your age, race, sex, gender, religious, or political positions are, make this the time you take back your power. And there is no better way to do that than to start by rethinking failure.

ABOUT THE AUTHOR

Early in life, J. H. Wright determined to take control of his future by traveling the road of entrepreneurship. He built several successful businesses from the ground up, until he defined the ones that would allow him to live comfortably while experiencing the full enjoyment of serving others.

If you are looking to accelerate your road to success, he offers you various strategies that although universal, can be customized for the unique style you require in pursuing your personal endeavors. Whether you seek success in business, financial, personal, social life, or combinations thereof, you need individuality, direction, and commitment to obtain these goals.

It is his honor not only to share, but to help other's fulfill their dreams. Whether those dreams are serving your immediate neighborhood, or to serve the world, strategic planning is a must. Expertise has shown him that there is nothing like knowing you are in control of your life and the depth of happiness you choose to experience.

J. H. Wright will help guide you into your most creative powers, taking you to the limits of your deepest desires.

www.ingramcontent.com/pod-product-compliance
Lightning Source LLC
LaVergne TN
LVHW051845080426
835512LV00018B/3081